EASY ORIGAMI

Fumiaki Shingu

Mud Puddle Books
NEW YORK

Easy Origami
Created by Fumiaki Shingu

© 2007 by Mud Puddle Books, Inc.

Mud Puddle Books, Inc.
54 W. 21st Street
Suite 601
New York, NY 10010
info@mudpuddlebooks.com

ISBN: 978-1-60311-000-6

Printed and bound in China

CONTENTS

★ Very Easy   ★★ Easy   ★★★ More Difficult

INTRODUCTION

THE MAGICAL WORLD OF ORIGAMI

PICTURE A SQUARE PIECE OF PAPER.

Imagine that square piece of paper turning into an animal, a flower, a box or something that moves.

This is the timeless appeal of origami, the Japanese art of paper folding. Origami has been captivating people and holding them spellbound for more than a thousand years. It's believed that by folding, decorating and playing with paper you cultivate your creativity and spark your imagination.

It's easy to master the techniques of origami and, by practicing as much as you can, you develop your skills and quickly move on to more advanced steps and projects.

This book can be used by beginners and experts alike. The projects are classified according to their level of difficulty. Children and adults will readily find projects that match their skills.

It makes me very happy to share my origami experiences with you and I would be so pleased if my origami techniques provide you with joy and delight.

—Fumiaki Shingu
Tokyo 2006

EXPLANATION OF DIAGRAMS

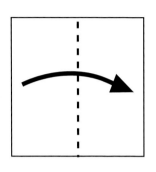 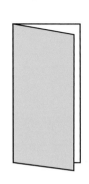

Fold on the dotted line.

Fold backward on the dotted line.

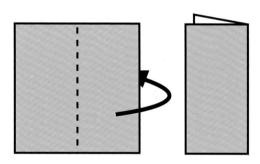

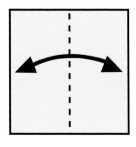 

Fold to make a crease and fold back.

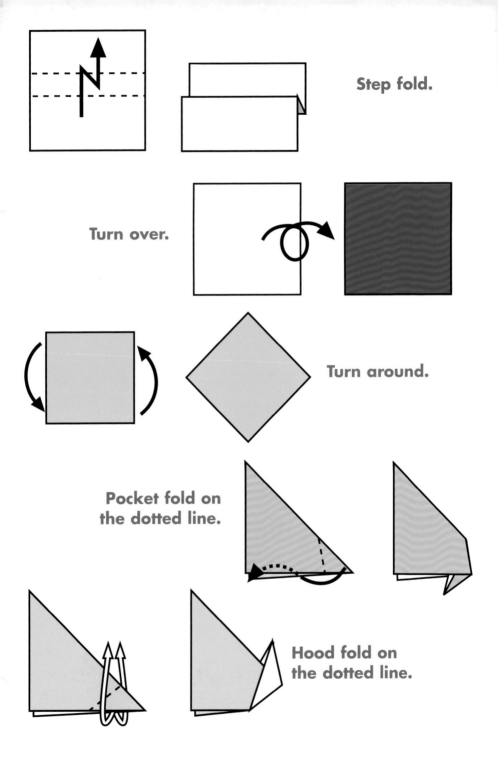

Step fold.

Turn over.

Turn around.

Pocket fold on the dotted line.

Hood fold on the dotted line.

FOLDING TECHNIQUES

Take time to practice and master the three basic folds described here. They are used throughout this book and will allow you to create the beautiful projects that follow.

Step Fold

❶ Fold on the dotted lines as if you were making a stair.

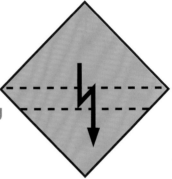

❷ First fold up on the dotted line.

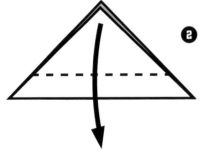

❸ Then fold back down on the other dotted line to complete the step fold.

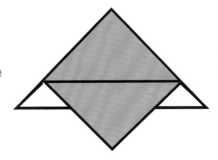

Pocket Fold

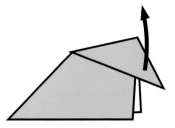

❶ Fold to make a crease.

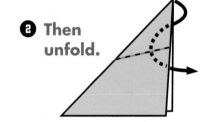

❷ Then unfold.

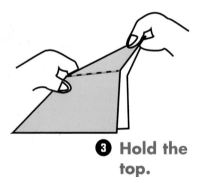

❸ Hold the top.

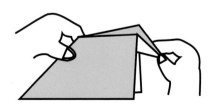

❹ And tuck in.

Hood Fold

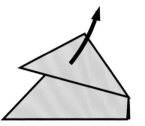

❶ Fold to make a crease.

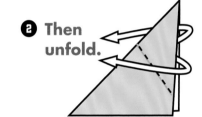

❷ Then unfold.

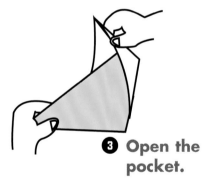

❸ Open the pocket.

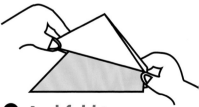

❹ And fold to cover the top.

CAT FACE ★

❶ Fold in half.

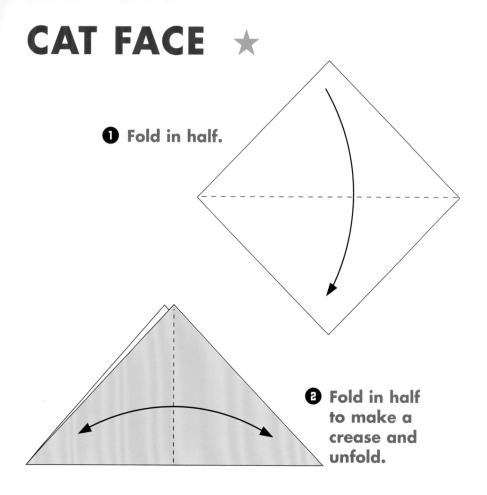

❷ Fold in half to make a crease and unfold.

❸ Fold on the dotted lines.

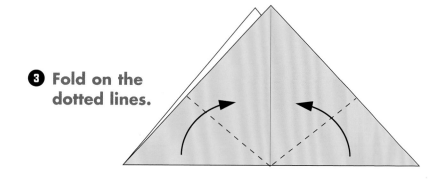

10

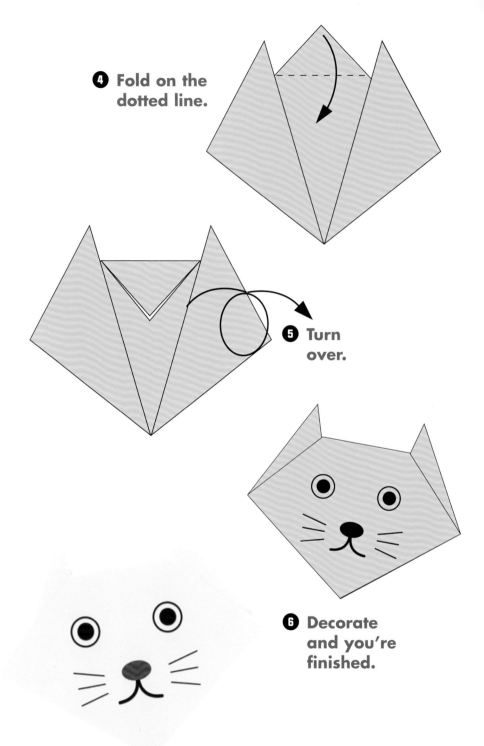

4 Fold on the dotted line.

5 Turn over.

6 Decorate and you're finished.

DOG FACE ★

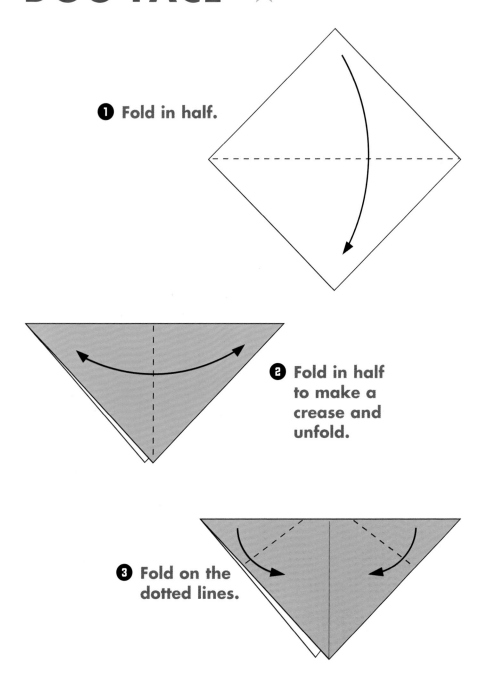

1 Fold in half.

2 Fold in half to make a crease and unfold.

3 Fold on the dotted lines.

4 Fold on the dotted line.

5 Fold on the dotted line.

6 Decorate and you're finished.

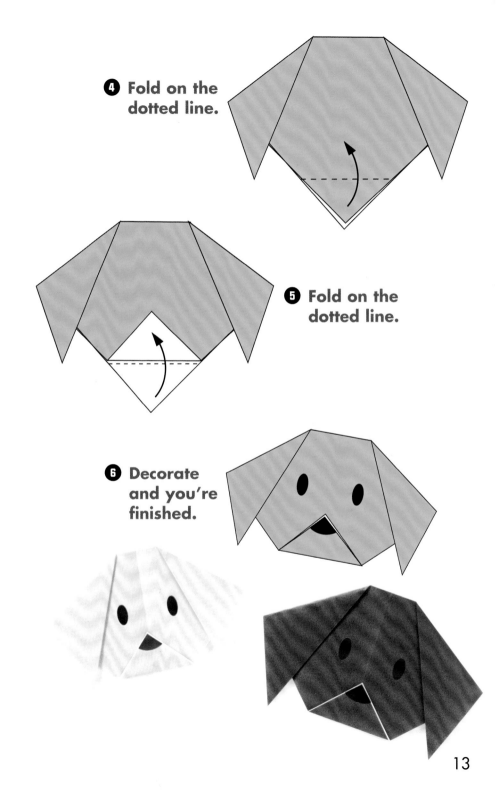

FLOWER ★★

LEAVES:

1 Fold in half to make a crease and unfold.

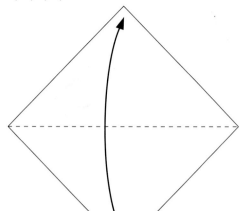

2 Fold on the dotted lines to meet the center line.

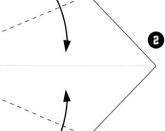

3 Fold on the dotted lines to meet the center line.

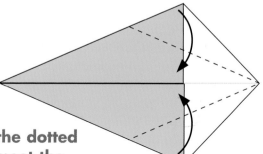

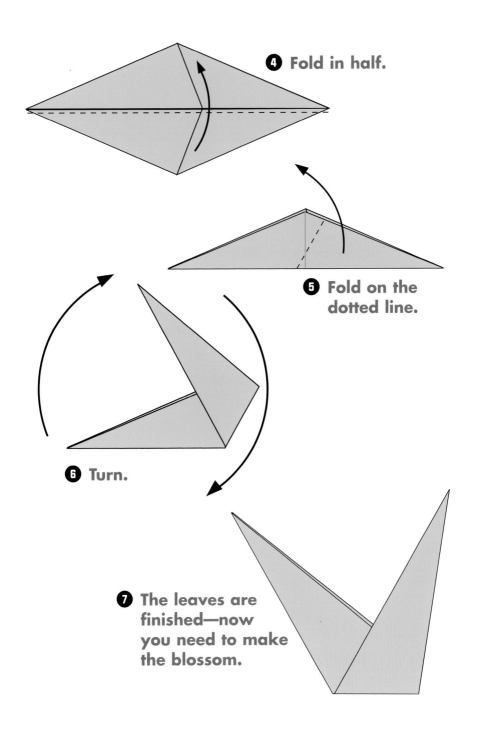

❹ Fold in half.

❺ Fold on the dotted line.

❻ Turn.

❼ The leaves are finished—now you need to make the blossom.

15

BLOSSOM:

1 Fold in half to make a crease and unfold.

2 Fold on the dotted lines to meet the center line.

3 Fold on the dotted lines.

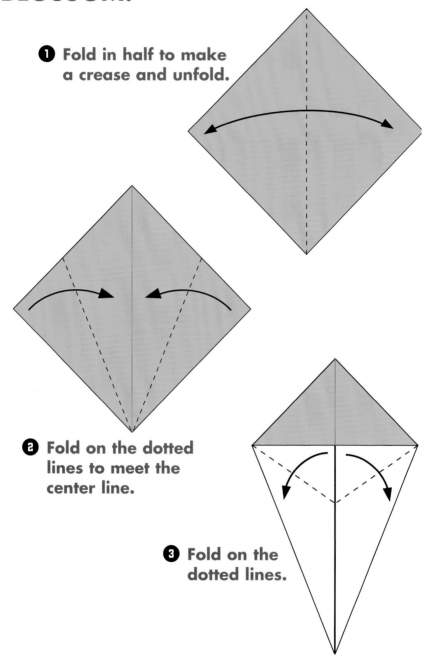

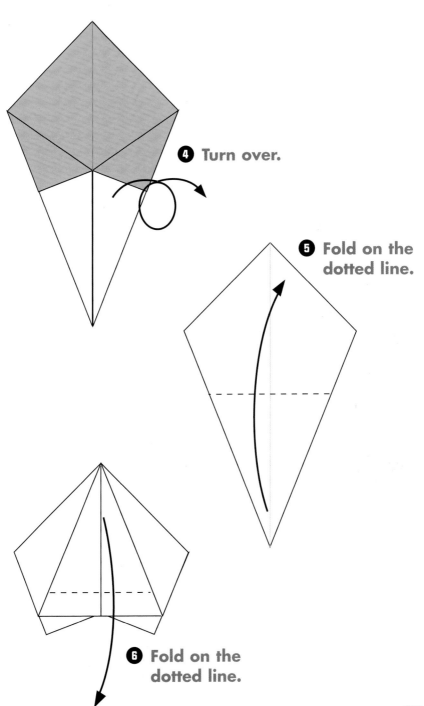

4 Turn over.

5 Fold on the dotted line.

6 Fold on the dotted line.

17

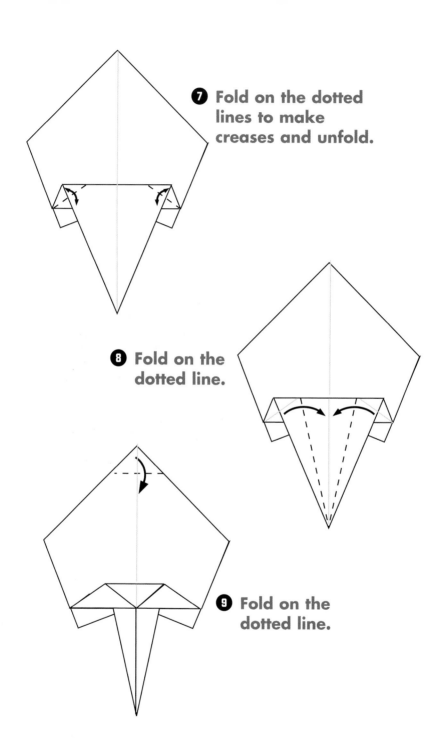

7 Fold on the dotted lines to make creases and unfold.

8 Fold on the dotted line.

9 Fold on the dotted line.

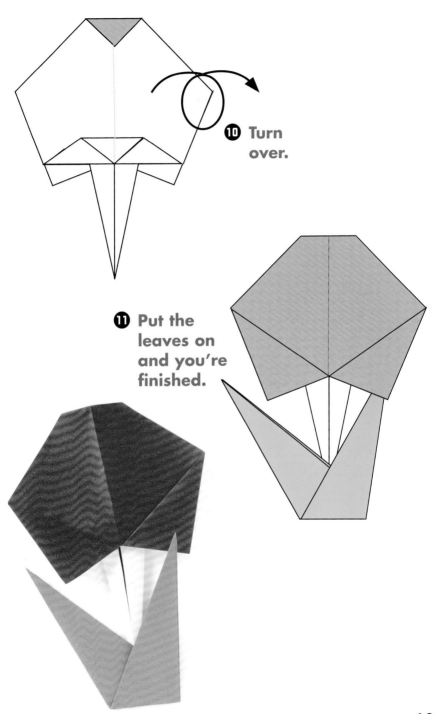

⑩ Turn over.

⑪ Put the leaves on and you're finished.

HOUSE ★★

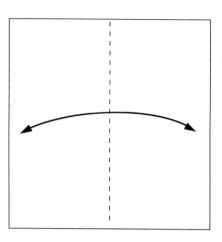

① Fold in half to make a crease and unfold.

② Fold on the dotted lines to meet the center line.

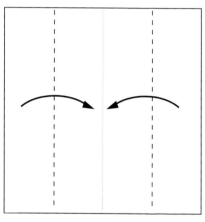

③ Fold on the dotted lines.

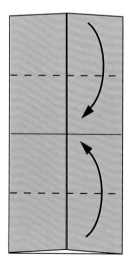

④ Unfold.

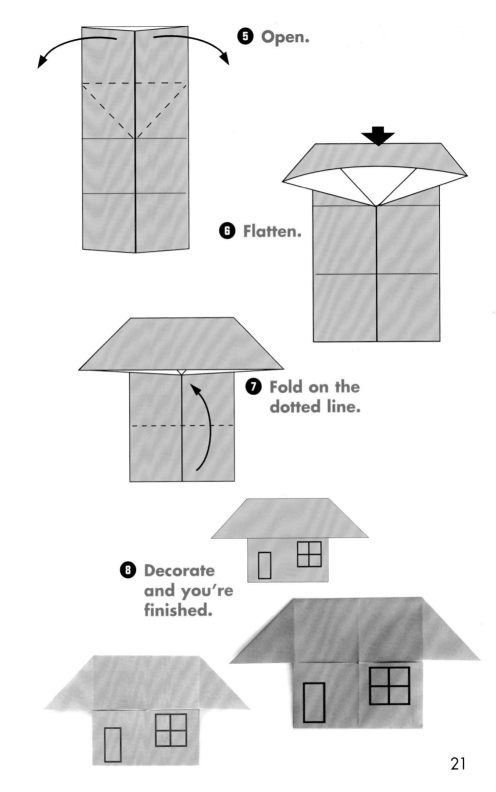

❺ Open.

❻ Flatten.

❼ Fold on the dotted line.

❽ Decorate and you're finished.

21

CAR ★★

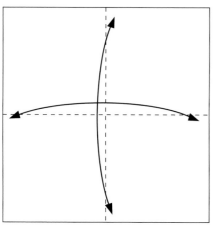

❶ Fold on the dotted lines to make creases and unfold.

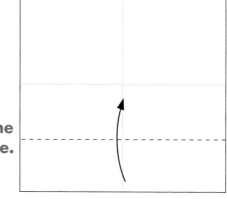

❷ Fold on the dotted line.

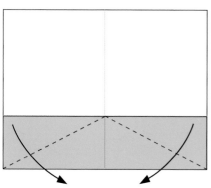

❸ Fold on the dotted lines.

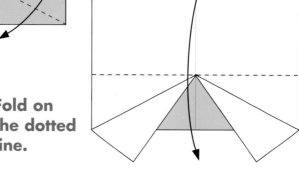

❹ Fold on the dotted line.

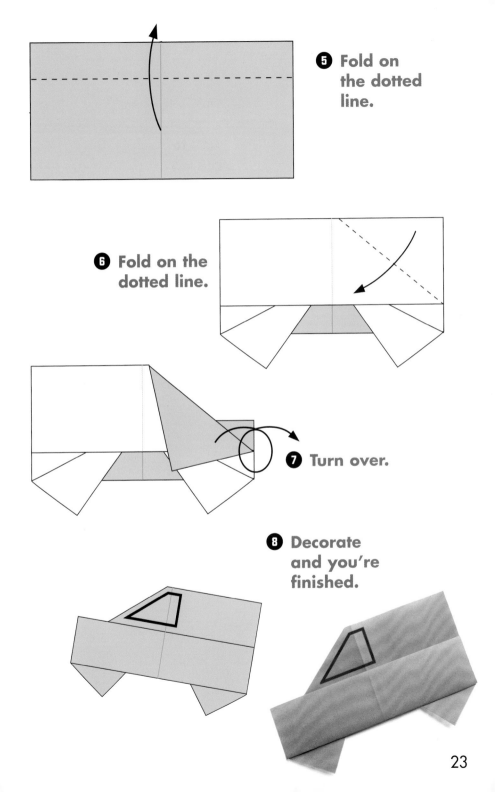

5 Fold on the dotted line.

6 Fold on the dotted line.

7 Turn over.

8 Decorate and you're finished.

BOAT ★★

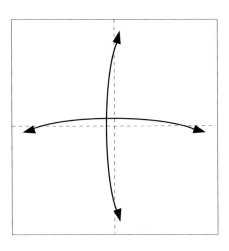

1 Fold on the dotted lines to make creases and unfold.

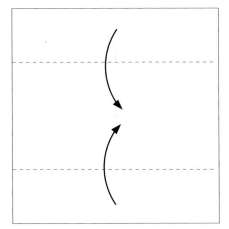

2 Fold on the dotted lines to meet the center line.

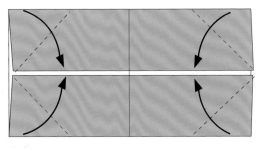

3 Fold on the dotted lines.

4 Fold on the dotted lines.

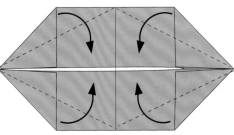

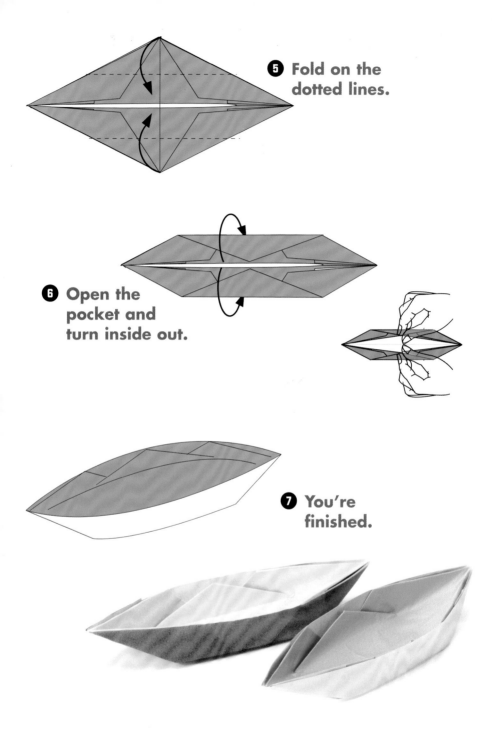

5 Fold on the dotted lines.

6 Open the pocket and turn inside out.

7 You're finished.

FLAPPING BUTTERFLY

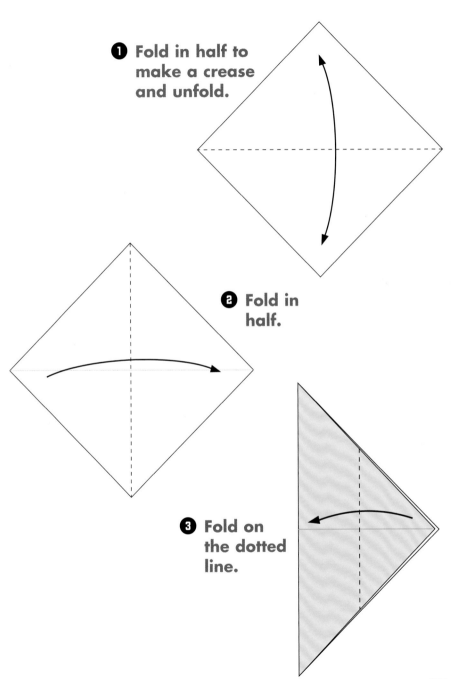

1 Fold in half to make a crease and unfold.

2 Fold in half.

3 Fold on the dotted line.

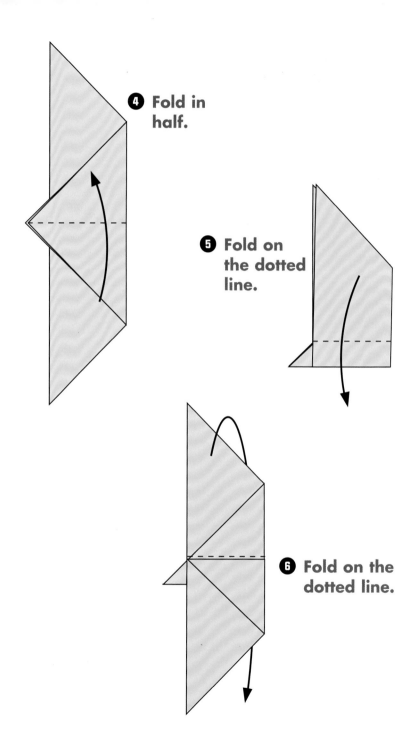

❹ Fold in half.

❺ Fold on the dotted line.

❻ Fold on the dotted line.

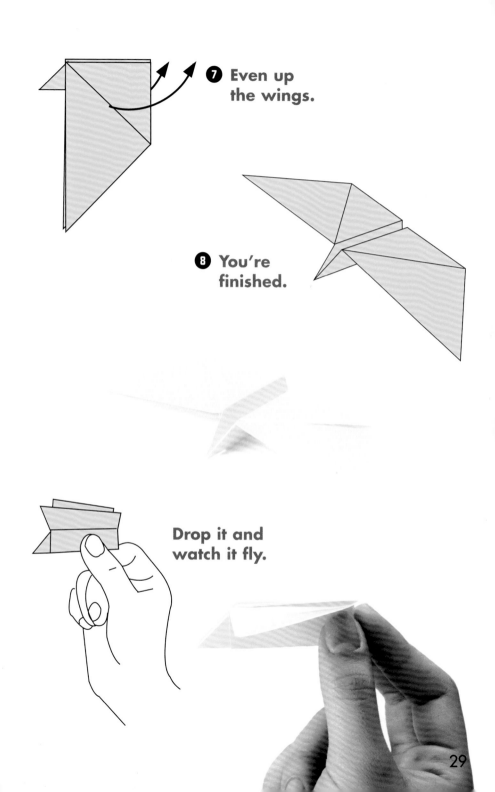

7 Even up the wings.

8 You're finished.

Drop it and watch it fly.

29

THUMPING HEART ★★★

❶ Fold on the dotted lines to make creases and unfold.

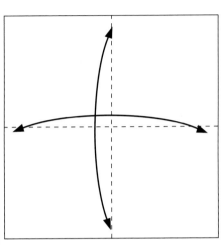

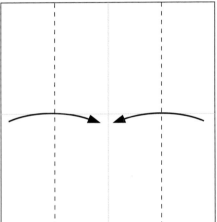

❷ Fold on the dotted lines to meet the center line.

❸ Turn over.

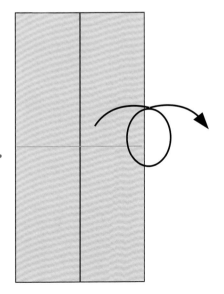

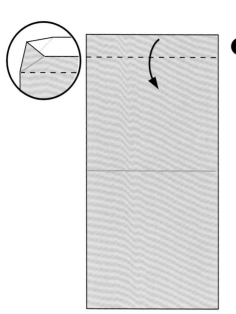

❹ Fold on the dotted line.

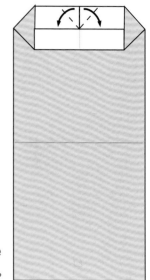

❺ Fold on the dotted line.

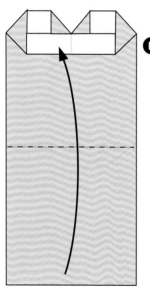

❻ Fold on the dotted line.

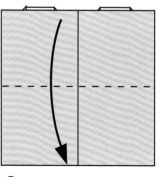

❼ Fold on the dotted line.

8 Fold and fold back.

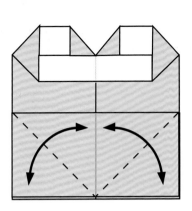

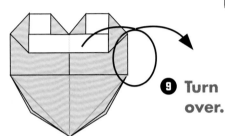

9 Turn over.

10 You're finished.

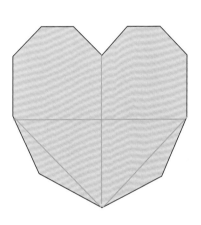

Pinch both sides to make the heart throb.

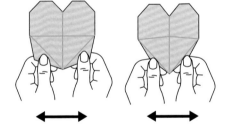

JUMPING FROG

1 Fold in half to make a crease and unfold.

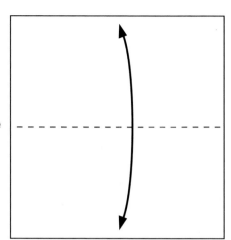

2 Fold in half.

3 Fold on the dotted line to make a crease and unfold.

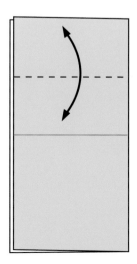

❹ Fold to make creases and unfold.

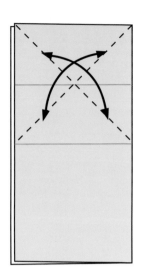

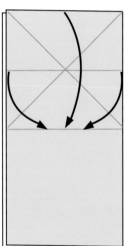

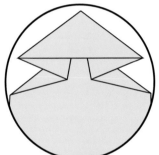

❺ Fold on the dotted lines.

❻ Fold on the dotted line.

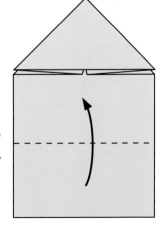

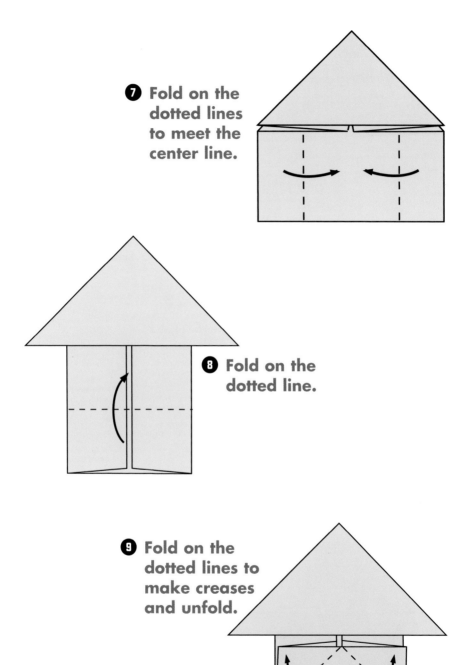

❼ Fold on the dotted lines to meet the center line.

❽ Fold on the dotted line.

❾ Fold on the dotted lines to make creases and unfold.

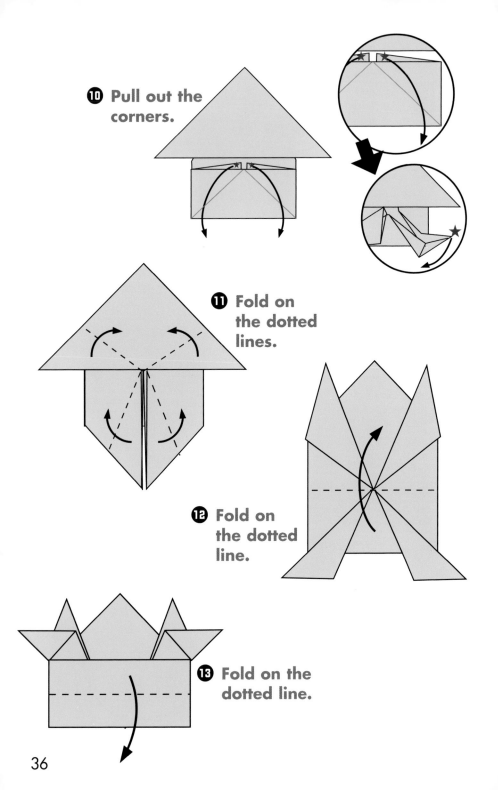

10 Pull out the corners.

11 Fold on the dotted lines.

12 Fold on the dotted line.

13 Fold on the dotted line.

36

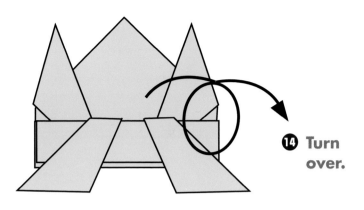

⓮ Turn over.

⓯ Decorate and you're finished.

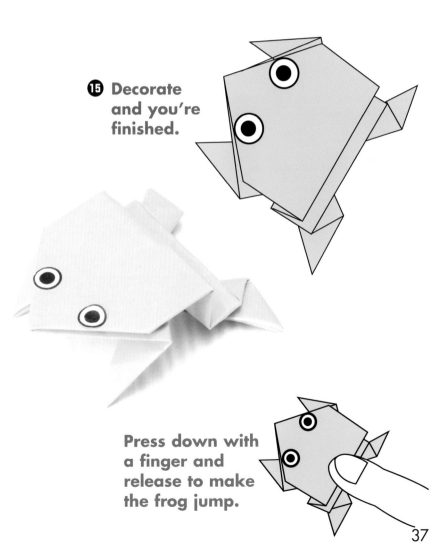

Press down with a finger and release to make the frog jump.

ELEPHANT ★★★

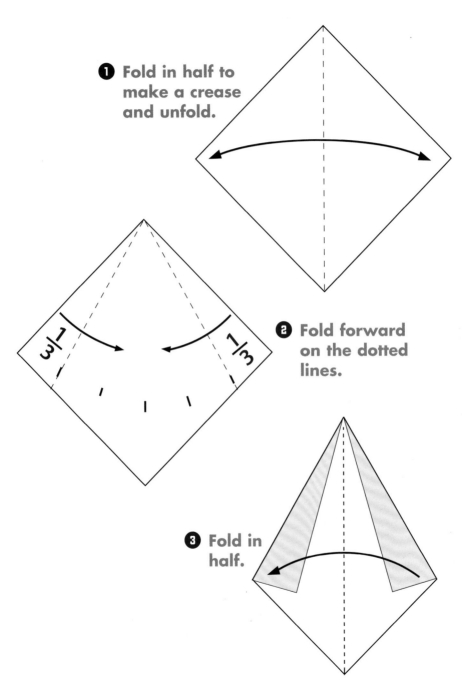

1 Fold in half to make a crease and unfold.

2 Fold forward on the dotted lines.

$\frac{1}{3}$ $\frac{1}{3}$

3 Fold in half.

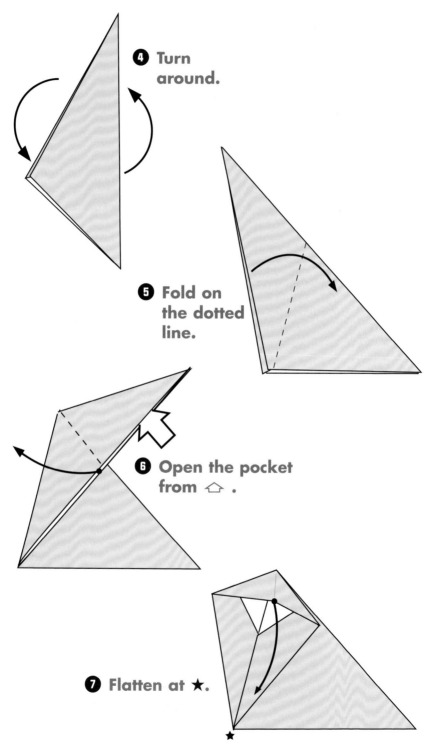

4 Turn around.

5 Fold on the dotted line.

6 Open the pocket from ⌂ .

7 Flatten at ★.

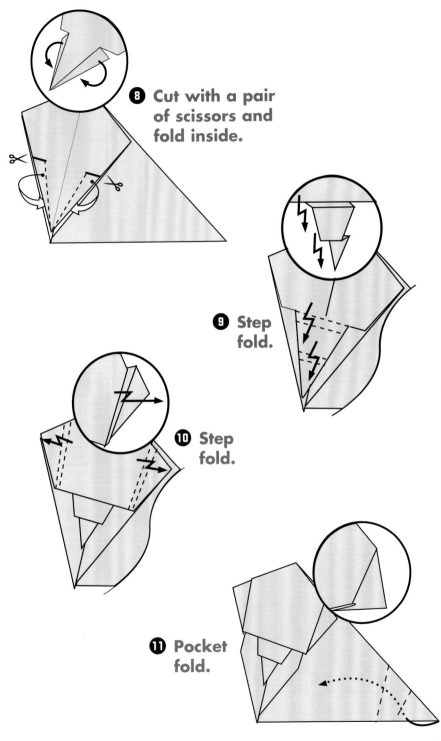

8 Cut with a pair of scissors and fold inside.

9 Step fold.

10 Step fold.

11 Pocket fold.

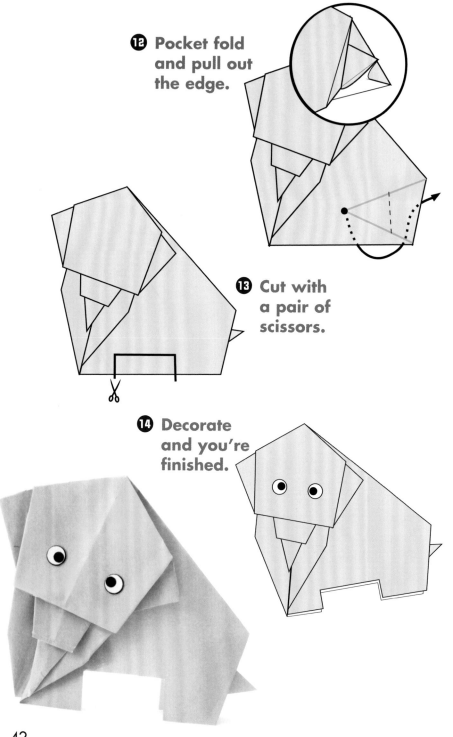

12 Pocket fold
and pull out
the edge.

13 Cut with
a pair of
scissors.

14 Decorate
and you're
finished.

SWAN ★★

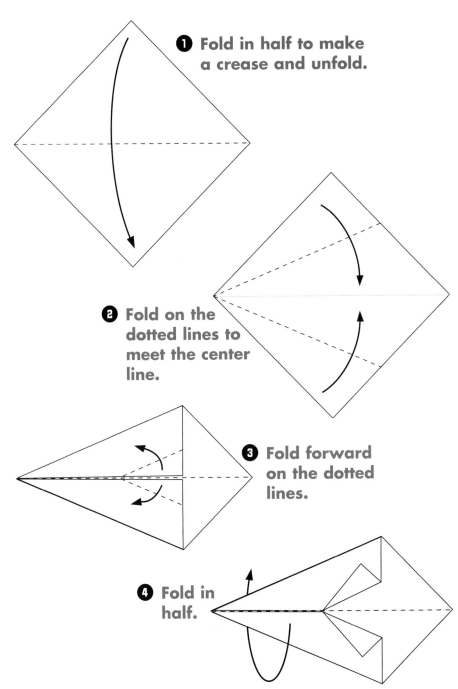

1 Fold in half to make a crease and unfold.

2 Fold on the dotted lines to meet the center line.

3 Fold forward on the dotted lines.

4 Fold in half.

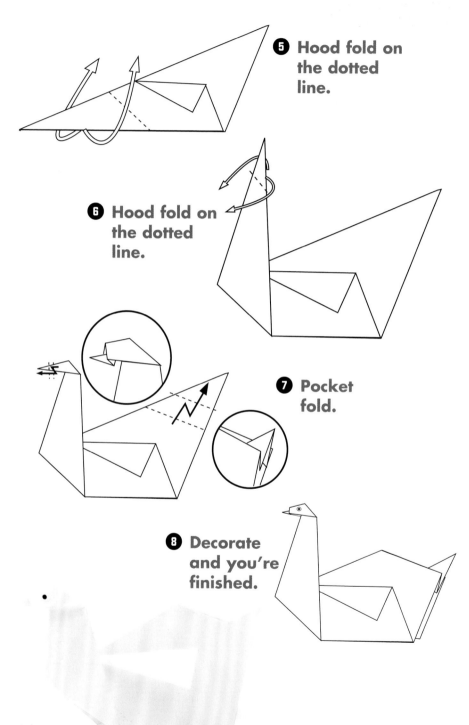

5 Hood fold on the dotted line.

6 Hood fold on the dotted line.

7 Pocket fold.

8 Decorate and you're finished.

GIRAFFE ★★

1 Fold in half to make a crease and unfold.

2 Fold on the dotted lines to meet the center line.

3 Fold in half.

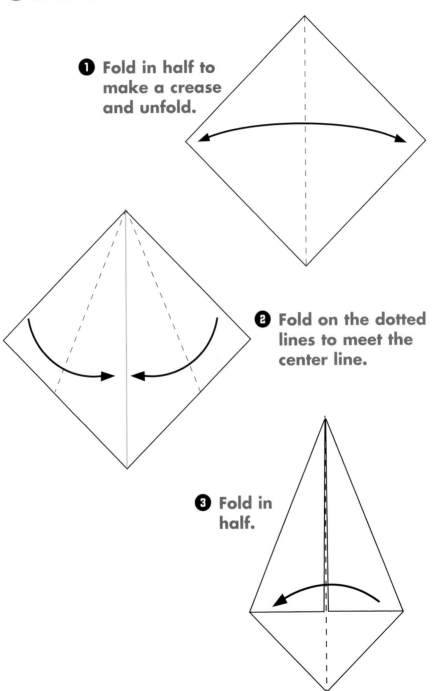

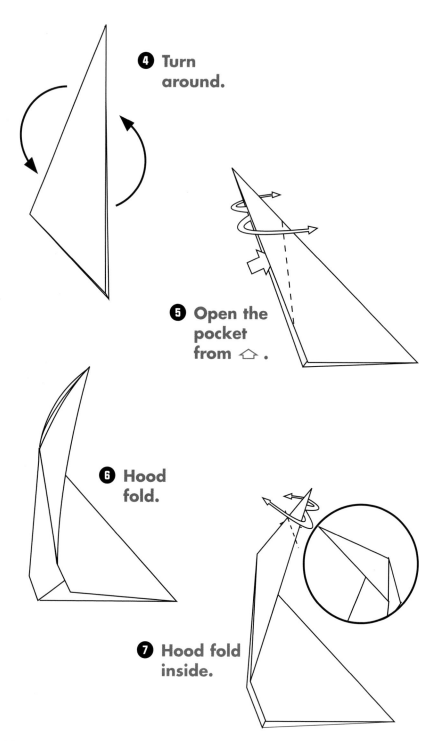

4 Turn around.

5 Open the pocket from ⌂.

6 Hood fold.

7 Hood fold inside.

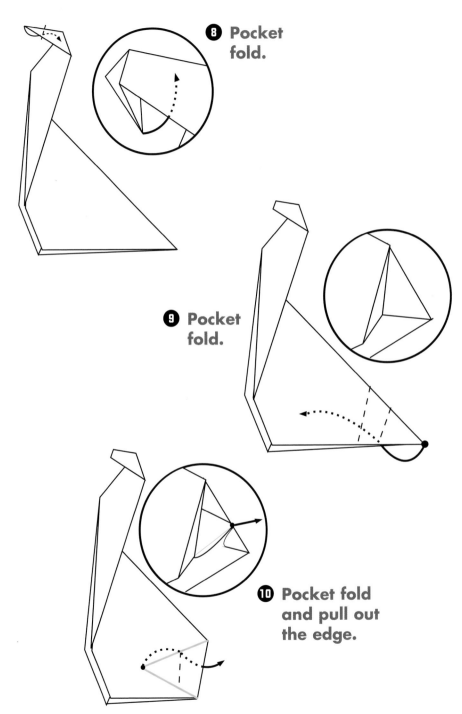

8 Pocket fold.

9 Pocket fold.

10 Pocket fold and pull out the edge.

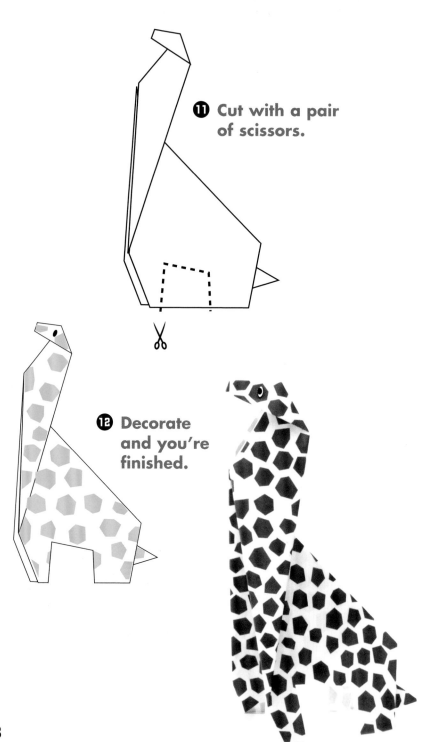

11 Cut with a pair of scissors.

12 Decorate and you're finished.

LADY BUG ★★

❶ Fold on the dotted lines to meet the center line.

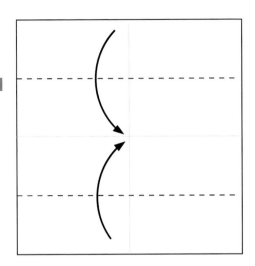

❷ Fold on the dotted lines to meet the center line and unfold.

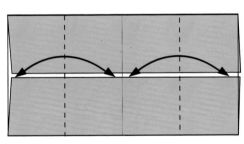

❸ Fold on the dotted lines.

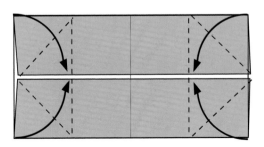

4 Open the pocket from ⌂ and flatten.

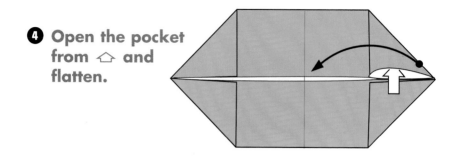

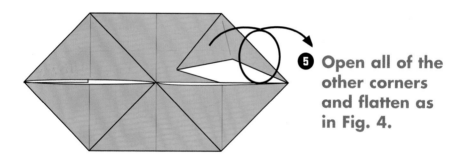

5 Open all of the other corners and flatten as in Fig. 4.

6 Fold on the dotted lines.

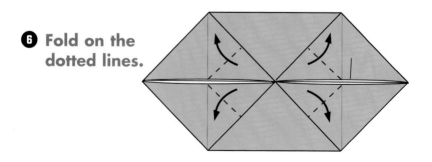

❼ Fold on the dotted lines.

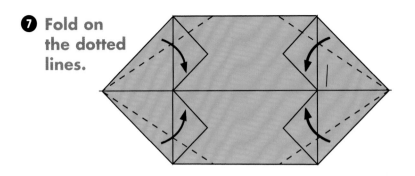

❽ Fold backward on the dotted lines.

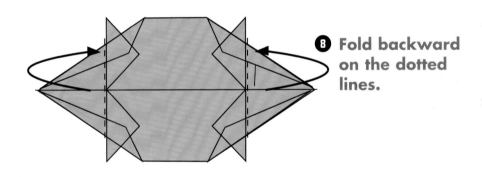

❾ Fold on the dotted line.

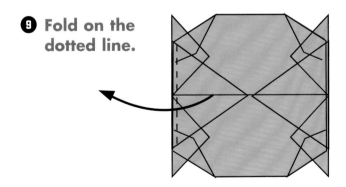

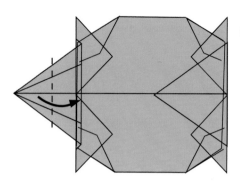

10 Fold backward on the dotted line.

11 Fold in half.

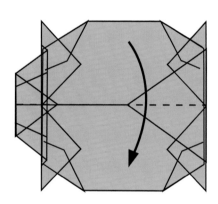

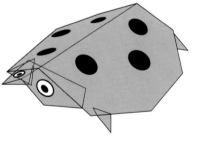

12 Decorate and you're finished.

SNOWMAN ★★

❶ Fold in half.

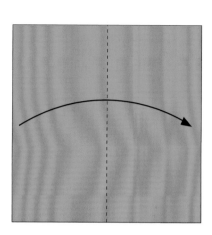

❷ Fold to make a crease and unfold.

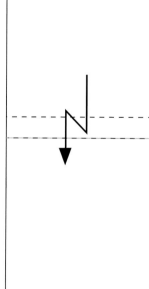

❸ Step fold forward on the dotted lines.

4 Fold on the dotted lines.

5 Fold on the dotted lines.

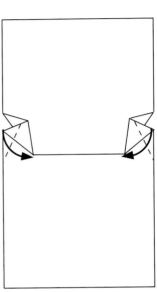

6 Fold on the dotted lines.

7 Turn over.

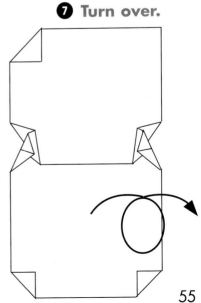

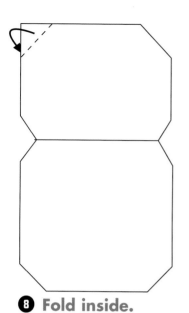

8 Fold inside.

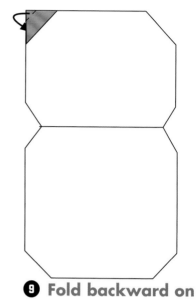

9 Fold backward on the dotted lines.

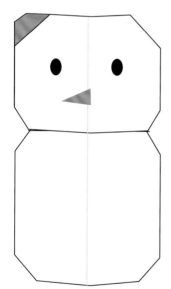

10 Fold in half, decorate and you're finished.

SANTA ★★★

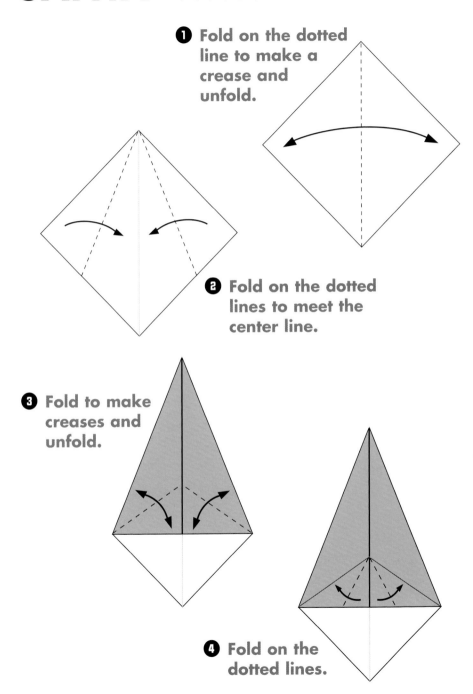

1 Fold on the dotted line to make a crease and unfold.

2 Fold on the dotted lines to meet the center line.

3 Fold to make creases and unfold.

4 Fold on the dotted lines.

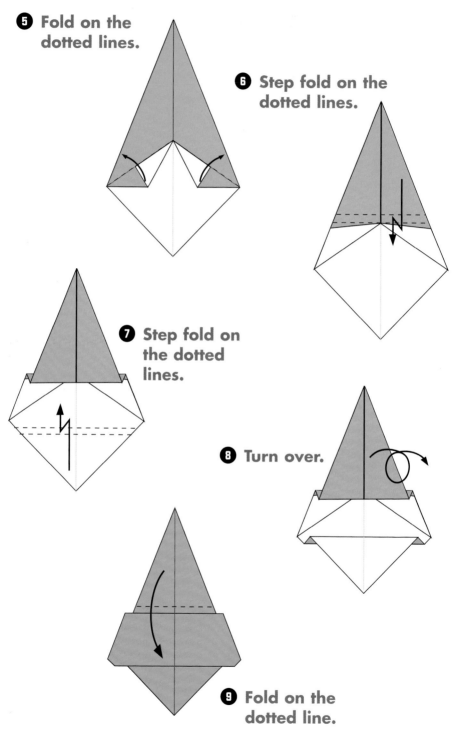

5 Fold on the dotted lines.

6 Step fold on the dotted lines.

7 Step fold on the dotted lines.

8 Turn over.

9 Fold on the dotted line.

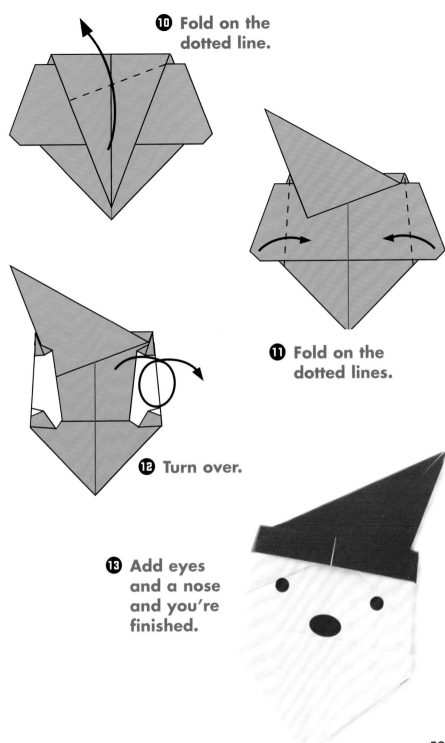

10 Fold on the dotted line.

11 Fold on the dotted lines.

12 Turn over.

13 Add eyes and a nose and you're finished.

BAT ★★★

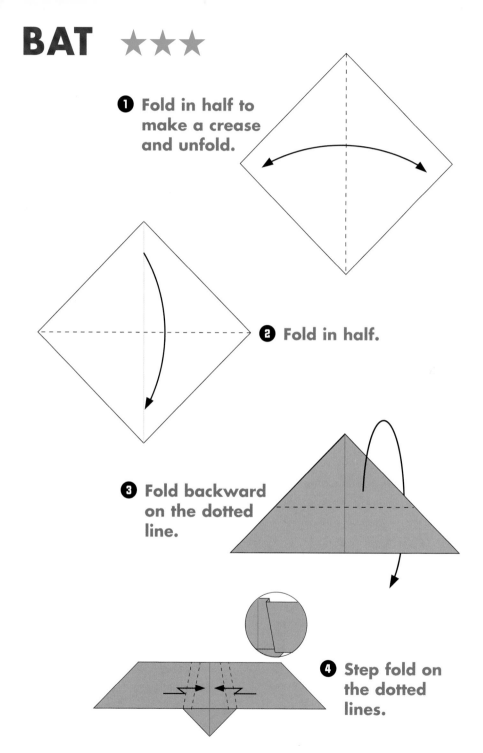

1 Fold in half to make a crease and unfold.

2 Fold in half.

3 Fold backward on the dotted line.

4 Step fold on the dotted lines.

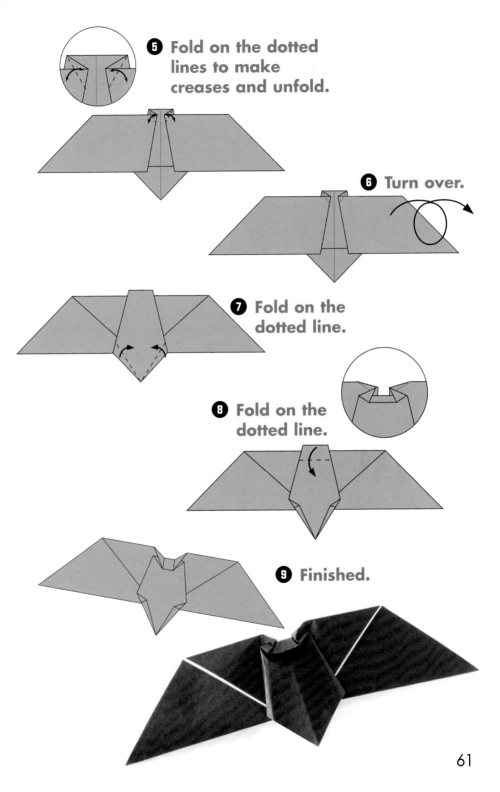

5 Fold on the dotted lines to make creases and unfold.

6 Turn over.

7 Fold on the dotted line.

8 Fold on the dotted line.

9 Finished.

61

GHOST ★★

1 Fold in half to make a crease and unfold.

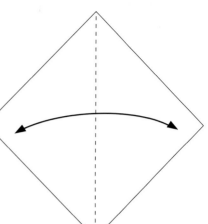

2 Fold on the dotted lines to meet the center line.

3 Fold on the dotted lines to meet the center line.

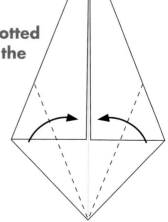

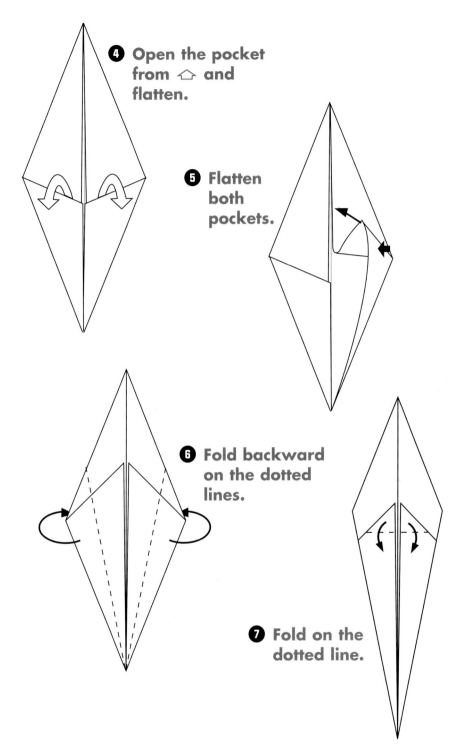

4 Open the pocket from △ and flatten.

5 Flatten both pockets.

6 Fold backward on the dotted lines.

7 Fold on the dotted line.

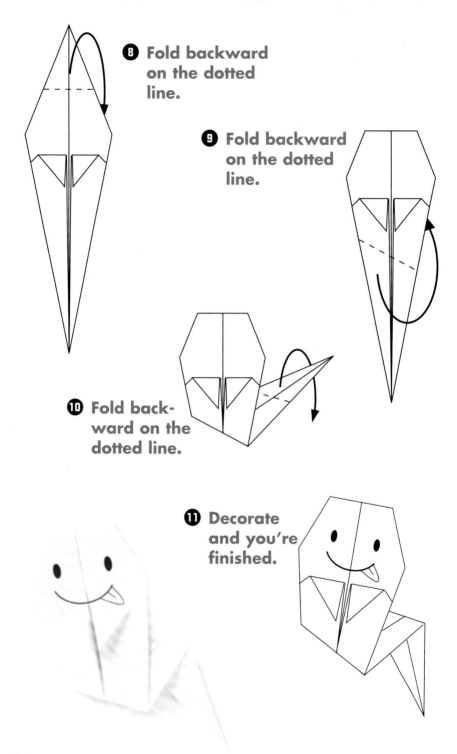

8 Fold backward on the dotted line.

9 Fold backward on the dotted line.

10 Fold backward on the dotted line.

11 Decorate and you're finished.

64